Shrugs, Shawls & Boleros

LION BRAND® HEARTLAND®

This sensationally soft, premium acrylic comes in heathered and tweedy shades inspired by the natural beauty of the American landscape. Its subtle shades suggest landmarks such as the Redwood Forest, the Everglades, and Yosemite National Park. Made in America, Heartland® is an easy-care medium/worsted weight yarn that is perfect for garments, afghans, and accessories. You'll love the beautiful look and comforting feel it gives these shrugs, shawls, and boleros.

I0866867

About Lion Brand® Yarn Company

Lion Brand® Yarn Company is a 5th generation, family-owned and operated business, and a beloved American brand since 1878. The company is devoted to inspiring and educating knitters and crocheters with yarns, patterns, how-tos, and ideas that elevate their yarn crafting experience.

LEISURE ARTS, INC.
Maumelle, Arkansas

CHEVRON LACE SHAWL

EASY

SIZE

About 18" x 58" (45.5 cm x 147.5 cm)

SHOPPING LIST

Yarn (Medium Weight) MEDIUM 4

LION BRAND® HEARTLAND® (Art. #136)

- ☐ #147 Hot Springs - 3 balls
  or color of your choice

Crochet Hook

LION BRAND® crochet hook

- ☐ Size J-10 (6 mm)
  or size needed for gauge

Additional Supplies

- ☐ LION BRAND® large-eyed blunt needle

GAUGE

2 ripples = 6" (15 cm) measured from peak to peak.

BE SURE TO CHECK YOUR GAUGE.

— STITCH GUIDE —

DOUBLE CROCHET 3 TOGETHER (abbreviated dc3tog)

(Yarn over, insert hook in next st and draw up a loop, yarn over, draw through 2 loops) 3 times, yarn over and draw through all 4 loops on hook – 2 sts decreased.

SINGLE CROCHET 3 TOGETHER (abbreviated sc3tog)

(Insert hook in next st and draw up a loop) 3 times, yarn over and draw through all 4 loops on hook – 2 sts decreased.

NOTES

1. Shawl is worked in a ripple crochet pattern. The ripple pattern is easy to do, but it's important to remember that you may need to work several rows before the ripple pattern becomes clear.
2. The ripple in this design is created by working dc3tog or sc3tog to form 'valleys' and (dc, ch 3, dc) or (sc, ch 1, sc) to form 'peaks'. In each row, take care to work dc3tog or sc3tog over the 3 sts in each 'valley' and (dc, ch 3, dc) or (sc, ch 1, sc) in the center sp of each 'peak.'

SHAWL

Ch 89.

Row 1: Dc in 5th ch from hook (beg ch counts as dc, ch 1), (ch 1, sk next ch, dc in next ch) twice, *ch 1, sk next ch, dc3tog over next 3 ch, (ch 1, sk next ch, dc in next ch) twice, ch 1, sk next ch, (dc, ch 3, dc) in next ch, (ch 1, sk next ch, dc in next ch) twice; rep from * to last 10 ch, ch 1, sk next ch, dc3tog over next 3 ch, (ch 1, sk next ch, dc in next ch) twice, ch 1, sk next ch, (dc, ch 1, dc) in last ch – 6 ripples.

Row 2: Ch 1, turn, sc in first dc, sc in next ch-1 sp, (ch 1, sc in next ch-1 sp) twice, ch 1, sc3tog over next (ch-1 sp, dc3tog, ch-1 sp), *(ch 1, sc in next ch-1 sp) twice, ch 1, (sc, ch 1, sc) in next ch-3 sp, (ch 1, sc in next ch-1 sp) twice, ch 1, sc3tog over next (ch-1 sp, dc3tog, ch-1 sp); rep from * to last 3 ch-1 sps, (ch 1, sc in next ch-1 sp) 3 times, sc in 3rd ch of beg ch-4.

Row 3: Ch 4 (beg ch counts as dc, ch 1), turn, dc in first sc, (ch 1, dc in next ch-1 sp) twice, *ch 1, dc3tog over next (ch-1 sp, sc3tog, ch-1 sp), (ch 1, dc in next ch-1 sp) twice, ch 1, (dc, ch 3, dc) in next ch-1 sp, (ch 1, dc in next ch-1 sp) twice; rep from * to last 4 ch-1 sps, ch 1, dc3tog over next (ch-1 sp, sc3tog, ch-1 sp), (ch 1, dc in next ch-1 sp) twice, ch 1, (dc, ch 1, dc) in last st.

Repeat Rows 2 and 3 until piece measures about 58" (147.5 cm) from beg, end with a Row 3 as the last row you work.
Fasten off.

FINISHING

Weave in ends.

FILET CROCHET SHAWL

EASY +

SIZES

Finished Width:
50" (127 cm), across top edge
Finished Length: 25" (63.5 cm)

SHOPPING LIST

Yarn (Medium Weight) MEDIUM 4

LION BRAND® HEARTLAND® (Art. #136)

- ☐ #144 Kenai Fjords - 2 balls
  or color of your choice

Crochet Hook

LION BRAND® crochet hook

- ☐ Size J-10 (6 mm)
  or size needed for gauge

Additional Supplies

- ☐ LION BRAND® stitch markers
- ☐ LION BRAND® large-eyed blunt needle

GAUGE

14 dc + 6 rows = about 4" (10 cm).
BE SURE TO CHECK YOUR GAUGE.

NOTES

1. Shawl is worked back and forth in rows beg at center top.
2. Markers are placed and increases are worked at markers to shape the Shawl.
3. An edging is worked around the outer edge of Shawl.

SHAWL

Wrap yarn around index finger. Insert hook into ring on finger, yarn over and draw up a loop. Carefully slip ring from finger and work the stitches of Row 1 into the ring.

Row 1: Ch 4 (counts as first dc, ch 1 in this row and in all following rows), dc in ring, (ch 1, dc in ring) 3 times – you will have 5 dc and 4 ch-1 sps. Gently but firmly, pull yarn tail to tighten center of ring.

Row 2: Ch 4, turn, dc in first dc, *ch 1, sk next ch-1 sp, (dc, ch 1, dc) in next dc; rep from * to turning ch-sp, ch 1, dc in turning ch-sp – 9 dc and 8 ch-1 sps.

Row 3: Ch 4, turn, sk first ch-1 sp, (dc, ch 1, dc) in next dc, *ch 1, sk next ch-1 sp, dc in next dc, ch 1, sk next ch-1 sp, (dc, ch 1, dc) in next dc; rep from * to turning ch-sp, ch 1, dc in turning ch-sp – 13 dc and 12 ch-1 sps.

Row 4: Ch 4, turn, sk first ch-1 sp, (dc, ch 1, dc) in next dc, *(ch 1, sk next ch-1 sp, dc in next dc) twice, ch 1, sk next ch-1 sp, (dc, ch 1, dc) in next dc; rep from * twice, ch 1, sk next ch-1 sp, dc in next dc, ch 1, dc in turning ch-sp – 17 dc and 16 ch-1 sps.

Row 5: Ch 4, turn, sk first ch-1 sp, dc in next st, ch 1, sk next ch-1 sp, (dc, ch 1, dc) in next dc, *(ch 1, sk next ch-1 sp, dc in next dc) 3 times, ch 1, sk next ch-1 sp, (dc, ch 1, dc) in next dc; rep from * twice, ch 1, sk next ch-1 sp, dc in next dc, ch 1, dc in turning ch-sp – 21 dc and 20 ch-1 sps.

Row 6: Ch 4, turn, sk first ch-1 sp, dc in next dc, ch 1, sk next ch-1 sp, (dc, ch 1, dc) in next dc, place a marker in last dc made, *(ch 1, sk next ch-1 sp, dc in next dc) 4 times, ch 1, sk next ch-1 sp, (dc, ch 1, dc) in next dc, place a marker in last dc made; rep from * twice, (ch 1, sk next ch-1 sp, dc in next dc) twice, ch 1, dc in turning ch-sp – 25 dc and 24 ch-1 sps.

Rows 7-10: Ch 4, turn, sk first ch-1 sp, dc in next dc, *(ch 1, sk next ch-sp, dc in next dc) to ch-sp before next marked dc, ch 1, sk next ch-sp, (dc, ch 1, dc) in marked dc, move marker to last dc made; rep from * 3 times, (ch 1, sk next ch-sp, dc in next dc) to turning ch-sp, ch 1, dc in turning ch-sp – 41 dc and 40 ch-1 sps at the end of Row 10.

Rows 11-14: Ch 5 (counts as first dc, ch 2), turn, sk first ch-sp, dc in next dc, *(ch 2, sk next ch-sp, dc in next dc) to ch-sp before next marked dc, ch 2, sk next ch-sp, dc in marked dc, move marker to last dc made; rep from * 3 times, (ch 2, sk next ch-sp, dc in next dc) to turning ch-sp, ch 2, dc in turning ch-sp – 41 dc and 40 ch-2 sps.

Rows 15 and 16: Ch 5 (counts as first dc, ch 2), turn, sk first ch-sp, dc in next dc, *(ch 2, sk next ch-sp, dc in next dc) to ch-sp before next marked dc, ch 2, sk next ch-sp, (dc, ch 2, dc) in marked dc, move marker to last dc made; rep from * 3 times, (ch 2, sk next ch-sp, dc in next dc) to turning ch-sp, ch 2, dc in turning ch-sp – 49 dc and 48 ch-2 sps at the end of Row 16.

Rows 17 and 18: Rep Row 11 twice.

Rows 19 and 20: Rep Rows 15 and 16 – 57 dc and 56 ch-2 sps at the end of Row 20.

Rows 21-24: Ch 6 (counts as first dc, ch 3), turn, sk first ch-sp, dc in next dc, *(ch 3, sk next ch-sp, dc in next dc) to ch-sp before next marked dc, ch 3, sk next ch-sp, dc in marked dc, move marker to last dc made; rep from * 3 times, (ch 3, sk next ch-sp, dc in next dc) to turning ch-sp, ch 3, dc in turning ch-sp – 57 dc and 56 ch-3 sps.

Rows 25 and 26: Ch 6 (counts as first dc, ch 3), turn, sk first ch-sp, dc in next dc, *(ch 3, sk next ch-sp, dc in next dc) to ch-sp before next marked dc, ch 3, sk next ch-sp, (dc, ch 3, dc) in marked dc, move marker to last dc made; rep from * 3 times, (ch 3, sk next ch-sp, dc in next dc) to turning ch-sp, ch 3, dc in turning ch-sp – 65 dc and 64 ch-3 sps at the end of Row 26.

Remove markers.

Rows 27-30: Ch 6 (counts as first dc, ch 3), turn, sk first ch-sp, dc in next dc, *ch 3, sk next ch-sp, dc in next dc; rep from * to turning ch-sp, ch 3, dc in turning ch-sp – 65 dc and 64 ch-3 sps.

Row 31: Ch 3 (counts as first dc), turn, 3 dc in first ch-sp, dc in next dc, *3 dc in next ch-sp, dc in next dc; rep from * to turning ch-sp, 4 dc in turning ch-sp – 257 dc.

Row 32: Ch 5 (counts as first dc, ch 2), turn, sk first 3 dc, dc in next dc, ch 2, sk next dc, dc in next dc, *(ch 2, sk next 2 dc, dc in next dc) twice, ch 2, sk next dc, dc in next dc; rep from * to 2 dc before turning ch, ch 2, sk next 2 dc, dc in top of turning ch – 97 dc and 96 ch-2 sps.

Row 33: Ch 3 (counts as first dc), turn, *2 dc in next ch-sp, dc in next dc, (ch 2, sk next ch-2 sp, dc in next dc) 4 times; rep from * to turning ch-sp, 3 dc in turning ch-sp – 137 dc and 76 ch-2 sps.

Row 34: Ch 5 (counts as first dc, ch 2), turn, sk first 3 dc, dc in next dc, (ch 2, sk next ch-2 sp, dc in next dc) 4 times, *ch 2, sk next 2 dc, dc in next dc, (ch 2, sk next ch-2 sp, dc in next dc) 4 times; rep from * to 2 dc before turning ch, ch 2, sk next 2 dc, dc in top of turning ch – 97 dc and 96 ch-2 sps.

Row 35: Rep Row 33.

Row 36: Ch 3 (counts as first dc), turn, sk first dc, dc in next 3 dc, 2 dc in next ch-sp, dc in next dc, (ch 2, dc in next dc) twice, 2 dc in next ch-sp, *dc in next 4 dc, 2 dc in next ch-sp, dc in next dc, (ch 2, dc in next dc) twice, 2 dc in next ch-sp; rep from * to 3 dc before turning ch, dc in next 3 dc, dc in top of turning ch – 209 dc and 38 ch-2 sps.

Row 37: Ch 3 (counts as first dc), turn, sk first dc, dc in next 6 dc, *(2 dc in next ch-2 sp, dc in next dc) twice, dc in next 9 dc; rep from * to turning ch, dc in top of turning ch – 289 dc.
Do not fasten off.

Edging

Rnd 1: Ch 1, turn, sc in each st to turning ch, 3 sc in turning ch-sp; work 2 sc in the end of each row all the way across top edge, 2 sc in corner; join with sl st in first sc.
Fasten off.

FINISHING

Weave in ends.

CONVERTIBLE FLOWER LACE SHRUG

Button it to create sleeves or a vest, or wear it unbuttoned as a shawl.

INTERMEDIATE

SIZE

About 18" x 50" (45.5 cm x 127 cm), including border

SHOPPING LIST

Yarn (Medium Weight)

MEDIUM 4

LION BRAND® HEARTLAND® (Art. #136)

- ☐ #130 Bryce Canyon - 3 balls
  or color of your choice

Crochet Hook

LION BRAND® crochet hook

- ☐ Size J-10 (6 mm)
  or size needed for gauge

Additional Supplies

- ☐ LION BRAND® large-eyed blunt needle
- ☐ 12 buttons, ¾" (19 mm) diameter

GAUGE

1 pattern rep = about 3½" (9 cm) in Flower Lace pattern.

Note: One pattern repeat consists of a "flower" (all clusters and chains between a pair of sc sts on each row).

BE SURE TO CHECK YOUR GAUGE.

STITCH GUIDE

3 TREBLE CROCHET CLUSTER (abbreviated 3-tr Cl)

(Yarn over) 2 times, insert hook in indicated st and draw up a loop, (yarn over and draw through 2 loops on hook) 2 times (2 loops rem on hook), *(yarn over) 2 times, insert hook in same st and draw up a loop, (yarn over and draw through 2 loops on hook) 2 times; rep from * once more, yarn over and draw through all loops on hook.

2 TREBLE CROCHET CLUSTER (abbreviated 2-tr Cl)

(Yarn over) 2 times, insert hook in indicated st and draw up a loop, (yarn over and draw through 2 loops on hook) 2 times (2 loops rem on hook), (yarn over) 2 times, insert hook in same st and draw up a loop, (yarn over and draw through 2 loops on hook) 2 times, yarn over and draw through all loops on hook.

NOTES

1. Shrug is worked as a rectangle in Flower Lace pattern. A border is worked around the entire outer edge of the rectangle.
2. Piece can be buttoned to wear as a sleeved shrug, vest, or left unbuttoned as a Shawl.
3. The ch-1 sps of the last rnds of the border are used as buttonholes. Buttons are sewn to opposite ends of the 2 long edges of the rectangle following Assembly Diagram, page 17.

SHRUG

Ch 42.

Beg Flower Lace Pattern

Row 1 (RS): Sc in 2nd ch from hook, *ch 3, sk next 3 ch, (3-tr Cl, ch 7, 3-tr Cl) in next ch, ch 3, sk next 3 ch, sc in next ch; rep from * across – you will have 5 pattern reps at the end of this row.

Row 2: Ch 5 (does not count as a st), turn, *3-tr Cl in 3rd ch of next ch-3 sp, ch 3, 2-tr Cl in top of 3-tr Cl just made, sc in center ch of next ch-7 sp, ch 3, 2-tr Cl in sc just made, 3-tr Cl in first ch of next ch-3 sp; rep from * across.

Row 3: Ch 3, turn, 2-tr Cl in top of first 3-tr Cl, ch 3, sk next 2-tr Cl, sc in next sc, ch 3, sk next 2-tr Cl, 3-tr Cl in next 3-tr Cl, *ch 7, 3-tr Cl in next 3-tr Cl, ch 3, sk next 2-tr Cl, sc in next sc, ch 3, sk next 2-tr Cl, 3-tr Cl in next 3-tr Cl; rep from * across.

Row 4: Ch 7 (counts as tr, ch 3), turn, 2-tr Cl in 4th ch from hook, 3-tr Cl in first ch of first ch-3 sp, 3-tr Cl in 3rd ch of next ch-3 sp, ch 3, 2-tr Cl in top of 3-tr Cl just made, *sc in center ch of next ch-7 sp, ch 3, 2-tr Cl in sc just made, 3-tr Cl in first ch of next ch-3 sp, 3-tr Cl in 3rd ch of next ch-3 sp, ch 3, 2-tr Cl in top of 3-tr Cl just made; rep from * across, tr in top of turning ch.

Row 5: Ch 1, turn, sc in first st, ch 3, 3-tr Cl in next 3-tr Cl, ch 7, 3-tr Cl in next 3-tr Cl, *ch 3, sk next ch-3 sp, sc in next sc, ch 3, 3-tr Cl in next 3-tr Cl, ch 7, 3-tr Cl in next 3-tr Cl; rep from * to turning ch-sp, ch 3, sc in 4th ch of turning ch.

Rep Rows 2-5 until piece measures about 48" (122 cm) from beg; end with a Row 3 as the last row you work.

Last Row: Ch 7 (counts as tr, ch 3), turn, 3-tr Cl in first ch of first ch-3 sp, 3-tr Cl in 3rd ch of next ch-3 sp, *ch 3, sc in center ch of next ch-7 sp, ch 3, 3-tr Cl in first ch of next ch-3 sp, 3-tr Cl in 3rd ch of next ch-3 sp; rep from * across, ch 3, tr in top of turning ch. Fasten off.

FINISHING

Border

Note: For Rnd 2 to work nicely, it is important to work an odd number of sts across each of the 4 edges of the rectangle. Try to work the same odd number of sts across both short edges, and the same odd number of sts across both long edges.

Rnd 1: Join yarn with sl st in any corner, ch 1 (does not count as a st), (hdc, sc) in same corner, *work an odd number of sc as evenly spaced as possible to next corner, (sc, hdc, sc) in corner; rep from * twice; work an odd number of sc as evenly spaced as possible to end of rnd, sc again in first corner; join with sl st in first hdc.

Rnd 2: Ch 1, (sc, hdc, sc) in same st as joining, *(ch 1, sk next st, sc in next st) to next (sc, hdc, sc) corner, ch 1, sk next sc, (sc, hdc, sc) in corner hdc; rep from * twice, (ch 1, sk next st, sc in next st) to last st, ch 1, sk last st; join with sl st in first sc.

Rnd 3: Sl st in each st to first ch-1 sp, (sl st, ch 1, sc) in first ch-1 sp, *ch 1, sk next st, sc in next ch-1 sp; rep from * around, working (sc, hdc, sc) in each corner hdc.
Fasten off.

Following Assembly Diagram, sew 6 buttons to each long edge of piece. Space the buttons evenly over the first 12" (30.5 cm) of opposite ends of the two long edges.

Weave in ends.

ASSEMBLY DIAGRAM

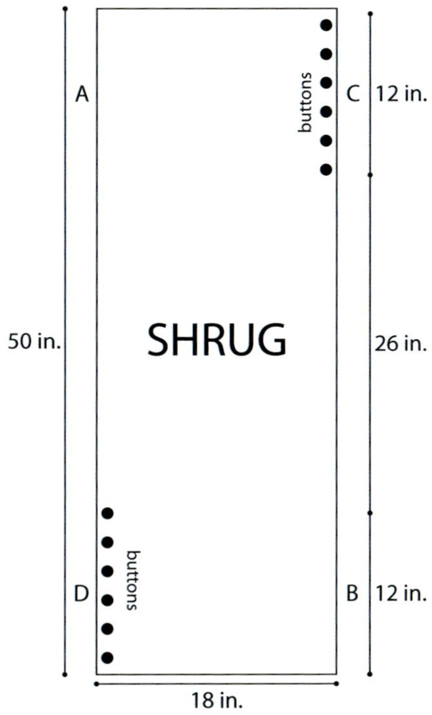

For sleeved Shrug, fold piece in half lengthwise then button C through A, and D through B.

For Vest, drape piece around your neck then button D through A.

LACY BOLERO

EASY

SIZES S/M{L/1X-2X/3X}

Finished Bust: 36{46-55}"/91.5{117-139.5} cm

Finished Length: 17½{18-18½}"/44.5{45.5-47} cm, not including edging

Note: Pattern is written for smallest size with changes for larger sizes in parentheses. When only one number is given, it applies to all sizes. To follow pattern more easily, circle all numbers pertaining to your size before beginning.

SHOPPING LIST

Yarn (Medium Weight) MEDIUM 4

LION BRAND® HEARTLAND® (Art. #136)

- ☐ #171 Cuyahoga Valley - 3{4-5} balls
  or color of your choice

Crochet Hooks

LION BRAND® crochet hook

- ☐ Size I-9 (5.5 mm)
- ☐ Size J-10 (6 mm)
  or sizes needed for gauge

Additional Supplies

- ☐ LION BRAND® large-eyed blunt needle

GAUGE
3 pattern reps = about 7" (18 cm); 13 rows = about 4" (10 cm) in Lacy Pattern using larger hook.

Note: One pattern rep consists of 4 sc and the following ch-sp(s).

BE SURE TO CHECK YOUR GAUGE.

STITCH GUIDE

REVERSE SINGLE CROCHET (abbreviated rev sc)
Single crochet worked from left to right (right to left, if left-handed). Insert hook into next stitch to the right (left), under loop on hook, and draw up a loop. Yarn over, draw through all loops on hook.

SINGLE CROCHET 2 CHAIN-SPACES TOGETHER (abbreviated sc2chsptog)
Insert hook under the 2 ch-sps from the 2 previous rows and draw up a loop, yarn over and draw through both loops on hook.

PATTERN STITCH

Lacy Pattern

Row 1 (RS): Sc in 2nd ch from hook and in next 4 ch, *ch 5, sk next 4 ch, sc in next 4 ch; rep from * to last ch, sc in last ch.

Row 2: Ch 1, turn, sc in first 5 sts, *ch 4, sk next ch-5 sp, sc in next 4 sts; rep from * to last st, sc in last st.

Row 3: Ch 1, turn, sc in first 5 sts, *ch 2, sc2chsptog, ch 2, sc in next 4 sts; rep from * to last st, sc in last st.

Row 4: Ch 1, turn, sc in first 5 sts, *ch 4, sk next 2 ch-2 sps, sc in next 4 sts; rep from * to last st, sc in last st.

Row 5: Ch 1, turn, sc in first st, *ch 5, sk next 4 sts, 4 sc in next ch-4 sp; rep from * to last 5 sts, ch 5, sk next 4 sts, sc in last st.

Row 6: Ch 1, turn, sc in first st, *ch 4, sk next ch-5 sp, sc in next 4 sts; rep from * to last ch-5 sp, ch 4, sk last ch-5 sp, sc in last st.

Row 7: Ch 1, turn, sc in first st, *ch 2, sc2chsptog, ch 2, sc in next 4 sts; rep from * to last ch-5 sp, ch 2, sc2chsptog, ch 2, sc in last st.

Row 8: Ch 1, turn, sc in first st, *ch 4, sk next 2 ch-2 sps, sc in next 4 sts; rep from * to last 2 ch-2 sps, ch 4, sk last 2 ch-2 sps, sc in last st.

Row 9: Ch 1, turn, sc in first st, 4 sc in next ch-4 sp, *ch 5, sk next 4 sts, 4 sc in next ch-4 sp; rep from * to last st, sc in last st.

Rep Rows 2-9 for Lacy Pattern.

NOTES

1. Bolero is made in sections. The Back is worked beg at neck edge. Then sts are worked across the opposite side of the Back foundation ch to beg Left and Right Fronts.
2. Sts are decreased at underarm(s) of Back and Fronts to complete short sleeve(s) and beg body.
3. Fronts are folded down over Back, sides seamed and edging worked around body and sleeve edges.

BACK

With larger hook, ch 71{87-103}.

Work in Lacy Pattern for 32 rows – 8¾{10¾-12¾} pattern reps.

Note: The last row you work should be a Row 8 of the Lacy pattern.

Decrease for Body

Row 1 (RS): Turn, sl st in first st, sl st in next 3 ch, ch 1, sc in next ch, *ch 5, sk next 4 sts, 4 sc in next ch-4 sp; rep from * to last 4-sc group, ch 5, sk next 4 sts, sc in first ch of next ch-4 sp; leave rem sts unworked – 7¾{9¾-11¾} pattern reps rem for body.

Beg with Row 6 of pattern, work in Lacy Pattern for 23{25-27} rows (for a total of 24{26-28} rows in body).
Fasten off.

LEFT FRONT

From RS with larger hook, working across opposite side of Back foundation ch, join yarn with sl st in first ch of 3rd{4th-5th} ch-4 sp from left edge, ch 14.

Row 1 (RS): Sc in 2nd ch from hook, ch 5, sk next 4 ch, sc in next 4 ch, ch 5, sk next 4 ch, 4 sc in same ch-4 sp as joining sl st, *ch 5, sk next 4 foundation ch, 4 sc in next ch-4 sp; rep from * across foundation ch to last 5 ch, ch 4, sk next 4 ch, sc in last ch – 4¾{5¾-6¾} pattern reps.

Beg with Row 6 of pattern, work in Lacy Pattern for 31 rows.

Note: The last row you work should be a Row 4 of the Lacy Pattern.

Decrease for Body

Row 1 (RS): Ch 1, turn, sc in first st, *ch 5, sk next 4 sts, 4 sc in next ch-4 sp; rep from * to last 5 sts, sc in next st; leave last 4 sts unworked – 4¼{5¼-6¼} pattern reps.

Row 2: Ch 1, turn, sc in first 5 sts, *ch 4, sk next ch-5 sp, sc in next 4 sts; rep from * to last ch-5 sp, ch 4, sk last ch-5 sp, sc in last st.

Row 3: Ch 1, turn, sc in first st, *ch 2, sc2chsptog, ch 2, sc in next 4 sts; rep from * to last st, sc in last st.

Row 4: Ch 1, turn, sc in first 5 sts, *ch 4, sk next 2 ch-2 sps, sc in next 4 sts; rep from * to last 2 ch-2 sps, ch 4, sk last 2 ch-2 sps, sc in last st.

Row 5: Ch 1, turn, sc in first st, 4 sc in next ch-4 sp, *ch 5, sk next 4 sts, 4 sc in next ch-4 sp; rep from * to last 5 sts, ch 5, sk next 4 sts, sc in last st.

Row 6: Ch 1, turn, sc in first st, *ch 4, sk next ch-5 sp, sc in next 4 sts; rep from * to last st, sc in last st.

Row 7: Ch 1, turn, sc in first 5 sts, *ch 2, sc2chsptog, ch 2, sc in next 4 sts; rep from * to last ch-4 sp, ch 2, sc2chsptog, ch 2, sc in last st.

Row 8: Ch 1, turn, sc in first st, *ch 4, sk next 2 ch-2 sps, sc in next 4 sts; rep from * to last st, sc in last st

Row 9: Ch 1, turn, sc in first st, *ch 5, sk next 4 sts, 4 sc in next ch-4 sp; rep from * to last st, sc in last st.

Rep Rows 2-9 until Left Front measures same as Back. Fasten off.

RIGHT FRONT

From RS with larger hook, working across opposite side of Back foundation ch, join yarn with sl st in last ch of 3rd{4th-5th} ch-4 sp from right edge, ch 13.
Fasten off.

From RS with larger hook, working across opposite side of Back foundation ch, join yarn with sl st in first ch at right edge.

Row 1 (RS): Ch 1, sc in same ch as joining, (ch 5, sk next 4 sts, 4 sc in next ch-4 sp) 3{4-5} times; working across ch-13, ch 5, sk first 4 ch, sc in next 4 ch, ch 5, sk next 4 ch, sc in last ch – 4¾{5¾-6¾} pattern reps.

Beg with Row 6 of pattern, work in Lacy Pattern for 31 rows.

Note: The last row you work should be a Row 4 of the Lacy Pattern.

Decrease for Body

Row 1 (RS): Turn, sl st in first 4 sts, ch 1, sc in next st, 4 sc in next ch-4 sp, *ch 5, sk next 4 sts, 4 sc in next ch-4 sp; rep from * to last 5 sts, ch 5, sk next 4 sts, sc in last st – 4¼{5¼-6¼} pattern reps.

Row 2: Ch 1, turn, sc in first st, *ch 4, sk next ch-5 sp, sc in next 4 sts; rep from * to last st, sc in last st.

Row 3: Ch 1, turn, sc in first 5 sts, *ch 2, sc2chsptog, ch 2, sc in next 4 sts; rep from * to last ch-4 sp, ch 2, sc2chsptog, ch 2, sc in last st.

Row 4: Ch 1, turn, sc in first st, *ch 4, sk next 2 ch-2 sps, sc in next 4 sts; rep from * to last st, sc in last st.

Row 5: Ch 1, turn, sc in first st, *ch 5, sk next 4 sts, 4 sc in next ch-4 sp; rep from * to last st, sc in last st.

Row 6: Ch 1, turn, sc in first 5 sts, *ch 4, sk next ch-5 sp, sc in next 4 sts; rep from * to last ch-5 sp, ch 4, sk last ch-5 sp, sc in last st.

Row 7: Ch 1, turn, sc in first st, *ch 2, sc2chsptog, ch 2, sc in next 4 sts; rep from * to last st, sc in last st.

Row 8: Ch 1, turn, sc in first 5 sts, *ch 4, sk next 2 ch-2 sps, sc in next 4 sts; rep from * to last 2 ch-2 sps, ch 4, sk last 2 ch-2 sps, sc in last st.

Row 9: Ch 1, turn, sc in first st, 4 sc in next ch-4 sp, *ch 5, sk next 4 sts, 4 sc in next ch-4 sp; rep from * to last 5 sts, ch 5, sk next 4 sts, sc in last st.

Rep Rows 2-9 until Right Front measures same as Back.
Fasten off.

FINISHING

Fold Fronts down over Back. Sew side and underarm seams.

Body Edging

From RS with smaller hook, join yarn with sl st in lower edge at either side seam.

Rnd 1: Ch 1, work sc as evenly spaced as possible all the way around outer edge; join with sl st in first sc.

Rnd 2: Ch 1, rev sc in each st around; join with sl st in beg ch. Fasten off.

Sleeve Edging

From RS with smaller hook, join yarn with sl st in sleeve edge at side seam.

Rnd 1: Ch 1, work sc as evenly spaced as possible around sleeve edge; join with sl st in first sc.

Rnd 2: Ch 1, rev sc in each st around; join with sl st in beg ch. Fasten off.

Weave in ends.

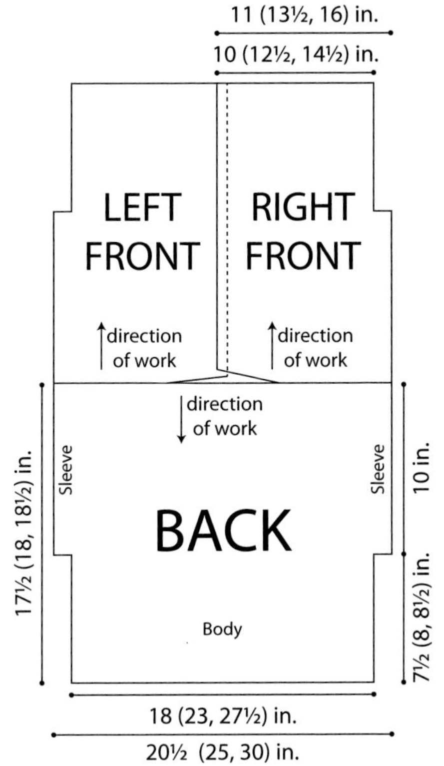

ROSY TWEED BOLERO

INTERMEDIATE +

SIZES S/M{L/1X-2X/3X}
Finished Bust: 36{46-56}"/91.5{117-142} cm
Finished Length: 13{14½-16½}"/33{37-42} cm at center back, not including edging

Note: Pattern is written for smallest size with changes for larger sizes in parentheses. When only one number is given, it applies to all sizes. To follow pattern more easily, circle all numbers pertaining to your size before beginning.

SHOPPING LIST

Yarn (Medium Weight) MEDIUM 4

LION BRAND® HEARTLAND® (Art. #136)

- ☐ #389 Isle Royale Tweed - 2{3-4} balls **or** color of your choice

Crochet Hook

LION BRAND® crochet hook

- ☐ Size I-9 (5.5 mm) **or** size needed for gauge

Additional Supplies

- ☐ LION BRAND® stitch markers
- ☐ LION BRAND® large-eyed blunt needle

GAUGE

2 pattern reps + 8½ rows = about 5" (12.5 cm).

Note: One pattern rep consists of (3 tr, ch 2, 3 sc, ch 2) **or** (3 dc, ch 2, 3 sc, ch 2).

BE SURE TO CHECK YOUR GAUGE.

STITCH GUIDE

SINGLE CROCHET 2 TOGETHER (abbreviated sc2tog)

(Insert hook in next st and draw up a loop) twice, yarn over and draw through all 3 loops on hook – 1 st decreased.

TREBLE CROCHET 2 TOGETHER (abbreviated tr2tog)

(Yarn over) twice, insert hook in next st and draw up a loop, (yarn over and draw through 2 loops) twice. (Yarn over) twice, insert hook in next st and draw up a loop, (yarn over, draw through 2 loops) twice, yarn over and draw through all 3 loops on hook – 1 st decreased.

NOTES

1. Bolero is made in 3 pieces: Back and 2 Fronts. The 2 Fronts are worked the same and the pattern stitch is reversible. When you put the Bolero together, simply flip one Front over so that it is the mirror image of the other Front.
2. Edgings are worked around armholes and outer edge of assembled Bolero.
3. When you see '0' repeats in an instruction, this means that you should not perform that particular instruction, just skip to the next part of the instruction.

BACK

Beg at lower edge, ch 65{81-97}.

Row 1 (RS): Dc in 4th ch from hook (3 skipped ch count as first dc), dc in next 3 ch, *ch 2, sk next ch, sc in next 3 ch, ch 2, sk next ch, dc in next 3 ch; rep from * to last 2 ch, dc in last 2 ch – you will have 49{61-73} sts and 14{18-22} ch-2 sps at the end of this row (for 7{9-11} pattern reps).

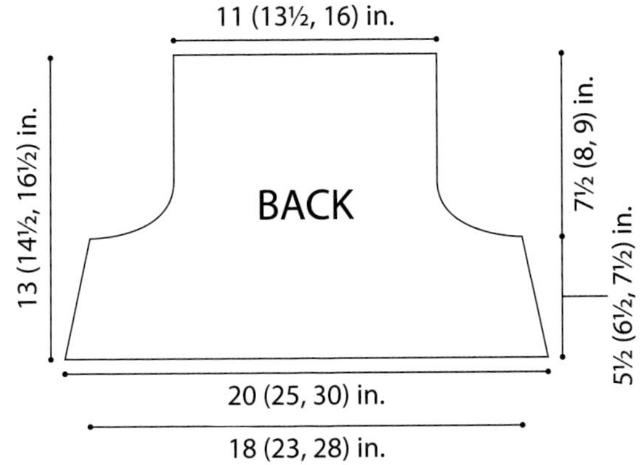

Row 2: Ch 1, turn, sc in first 5 sts, ch 2, sk next ch-2 sp, tr in next 3 sts, *ch 2, sk next ch-2 sp, sc in next 3 sts, ch 2, sk next ch-2 sp, tr in next 3 sts; rep from * to last ch-2 sp, ch 2, sk last ch-2 sp, sc in next 4 sts, sc in top of beg ch.

Row 3 (Decrease Row): Ch 3 (does not count as a st), turn, sk first st, tr in each st to first ch-2 sp, ch 2, sk next ch-2 sp, sc in next 3 sts, *ch 2, sk next ch-2 sp, tr in next 3 sts, ch 2, sk next ch-2 sp, sc in next 3 sts; rep from * to last ch-2 sp, ch 2, sk last ch-2 sp, tr in each st to last 2 sts, tr2tog – 47{59-71} sts and 14{18-22} ch-2 sps.

Row 4: Ch 1, turn, sc in each st to first ch-2 sp, ch 2, sk next ch-2 sp, tr in next 3 sts, *ch 2, sk next ch-2 sp, sc in next 3 sts, ch 2, sk next ch-2 sp, tr in next 3 sts; rep from * to last ch-2 sp, ch 2, sk last ch-2 sp, sc in each st to turning ch, leave turning ch unworked.

Rows 5-8: Rep Rows 3 and 4 twice – 43{55-67} sts and 14{18-22} ch-2 sps at the end of Row 7 (for 7{9-11} pattern reps).

Row 9: Ch 4 (counts as first tr), turn, tr in next st, ch 2, sk next ch-2 sp, sc in next 3 sts, *ch 2, sk next ch-2 sp, tr in next 3 sts, ch 2, sk next ch-2 sp, sc in next 3 sts; rep from * to last ch-2 sp, ch 2, sk last ch-2 sp, tr in last 2 sts.

Size S/M Only
Proceed to "Shape Armholes".

Sizes L/1X (2X/3X) Only
Row 10: Ch 1, turn, sc in each st to first ch-2 sp, ch 2, sk next ch-2 sp, tr in next 3 sts, *ch 2, sk next ch-2 sp, sc in next 3 sts, ch 2, sk next ch-2 sp, tr in next 3 sts; rep from * to last ch-2 sp, ch 2, sk last ch-2 sp, sc in last 2 sts.

Row 11: Rep Row 9.

Rep Rows 10 and 11 for 0{1} time(s) more.

Shape Armholes

Row 1 (WS): Turn, sl st in first 2 sts, ch 2, sk next ch-2 sp, tr in next 3 sts, *ch 2, sk next ch-2 sp, sc in next 3 sts, ch 2, sk next ch-2 sp, tr in next 3 sts; rep from * to last ch-2 sp, sk last ch-2 sp, tr in next st; leave turning ch unworked – 40{52-64} sts and 13{17-21} ch-2 sps.

Rows 2-3{(2-4)(2-5)}: Turn, sk first st, sl st in next 3 sts, ch 2, sk next ch-2 sp, tr in next 3 sts, *ch 2, sk next ch-2 sp, sc in next 3 sts, ch 2, sk next ch-2 sp, tr in next 3 sts; rep from * to last 2 ch-2 sps, sk next ch-2 sp, tr in next st; leave rem sts unworked – 28{34-40} sts (not counting sl sts) and 9{11-13} ch-2 sps at the end of Row 3{4-5}.

Row 4{5-6}: Ch 1, turn, sk first st, sc in next 3 sts, *ch 2, sk next ch-2 sp, tr in next 3 sts, ch 2, sk next ch-2 sp, sc in next 3 sts; rep from * to last ch-2 sp; leave last ch-2 sp unworked – 27{33-39} sts and 8{10-12} ch-2 sps.

Row 5{6-7}: Ch 4 (counts as first tr), turn, tr in next 2 sts, *ch 2, sk next ch-2 sp, sc in next 3 sts, ch 2, sk next ch-2 sp, tr in next 3 sts; rep from * across.

Row 6{7-8}: Ch 1, turn, sc in first 3 sts, ch 2, sk next ch-2 sp, tr in next 3 sts, *ch 2, sk next ch-2 sp, sc in next 3 sts, ch 2, sk next ch-2 sp, tr in next 3 sts; rep from * to last ch-2 sp, ch 2, sk last ch-2 sp, sc in next 2 sts, sc in top of turning ch.

Next 6 Rows: Rep last 2 rows 3 times.

Last Row: Ch 3 (counts as first dc), turn, dc in next 2 sts, *ch 1, sk next ch-2 sp, sc in next 3 sts, ch 1, sk next ch-2 sp, dc in next 3 sts; rep from * across.

Fasten off.

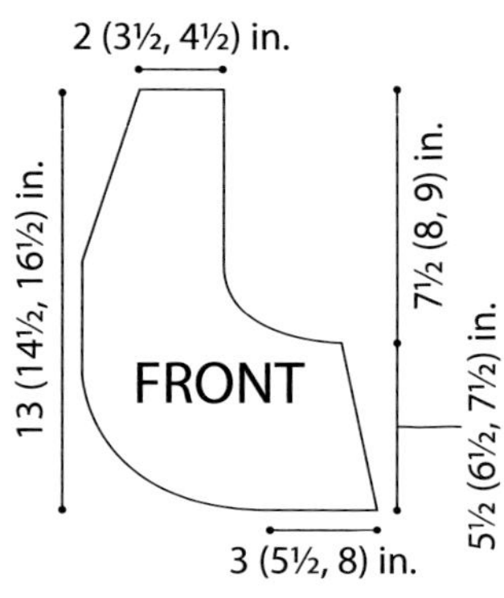

FRONTS (make 2)

Beg at lower edge, ch 10{18-26}.

Row 1: Sc in 2nd ch from hook and in next 2 ch, (ch 2, sk next ch, dc in next 3 ch, ch 2, sk next ch, sc in next 3 ch) 0{1-2} time(s), ch 2, sk next ch, dc in last 5 ch – you will have 8{14-20} sts and 1{3-5} ch-2 sps.

Row 2: Ch 1, turn, sc in first 5 sts, (ch 2, sk next ch-2 sp, tr in next 3 sts, ch 2, sk next ch-2 sp, sc in next 3 sts) 0{1-2} time(s), ch 2, sk next ch-2 sp, tr in next 2 sts, (tr, ch 2, dc) in last st – 9{15-21} sts and 2{4-6} ch-2 sps.

Row 3: Ch 9, turn, sc in 2nd ch from hook and in next 2 ch, ch 2, sk next 2 ch, tr in next 3 ch, ch 2, sk next ch-2 sp, sc in next 3 sts, (ch 2, sk next ch-2 sp, tr in next 3 sts, ch 2, sk next ch-2 sp, sc in next 3 sts) 0{1-2} time(s), ch 2, sk last ch-2 sp, tr in next 3 sts, tr2tog – 13{19-25} sts and 3{5-7} ch-2 sps.

Row 4: Ch 1, turn, sc in first 4 sts, (ch 2, sk next ch-2 sp, tr in next 3 sts, ch 2, sk next ch-2 sp, sc in next 3 sts) 1{2-3} time(s), ch 2, sk last ch-2 sp, tr in next 2 sts, (tr, ch 2, dc) in last st – 14{20-26} sts and 4{6-8} ch-2 sps.

Row 5: Ch 9, turn, sc in 2nd ch from hook and in next 2 ch, ch 2, sk next 2 ch, tr in next 3 ch, ch 2, sk next ch-2 sp, sc in next 3 sts, (ch 2, sk next ch-2 sp, tr in next 3 sts, ch 2, sk next ch-2 sp, sc in next 3 sts) 1{2-3} time(s), ch 2, sk last ch-2 sp, tr in next 2 sts, tr2tog – 18{24-30} sts and 5{7-9} ch-2 sps.

Row 6: Ch 1, turn, sc in first 3 sts, *ch 2, sk next ch-2 sp, tr in next 3 sts, ch 2, sk next ch-2 sp, sc in next 3 sts; rep from * to last ch-2 sp, ch 2, sk last ch-2 sp, tr in next 2 sts, (tr, ch 2, dc) in last st – 19{25-31} sts and 6{8-10} ch-2 sps.

Row 7: Ch 6, place marker in the 3rd ch of the ch-6 just made for front corner, turn, tr in 5th ch from hook (4 skipped ch count as first tr), tr in next ch, ch 2, sk next ch-2 sp, sc in next 3 sts, *ch 2, sk next ch-2 sp, tr in next 3 sts, ch 2, sk next ch-2 sp, sc in next 3 sts; rep from * to last ch-2 sp, ch 2, sk last ch-2 sp, tr in next st, tr2tog – 20{26-32} sts and 6{8-10} ch-2 sps.

Row 8: Ch 1, turn, sc in each st to first ch-2 sp, *ch 2, sk next ch-2 sp, tr in next 3 sts, ch 2, sk next ch-2 sp, sc in next 3 sts; rep from * across working last sc in top of turning ch.

Row 9: Ch 4 (counts as first tr), turn, tr in next 2 sts, ch 2, sk next ch-2 sp, sc in next 3 sts, *ch 2, sk next ch-2 sp, tr in next 3 sts, ch 2, sk next ch-2 sp, sc in next 3 sts; rep from * to last ch-2 sp, ch 2, sk last ch-2 sp, tr in last 2 sts.

Next 0{2-4} Rows: Rep Rows 8 and 9 for 0{1-2} time(s).

Shape Armhole and Neck

Row 1: Turn, sl st in first 2 sts, ch 2, sk next ch-2 sp, tr in next 3 sts, *ch 2, sk next ch-2 sp, sc in next 3 sts, ch 2, sk next ch-2 sp, tr in next 3 sts; rep from * to last ch-2 sp, ch 2, sk last ch-2 sp, sc in next 2 sts, sc in top of beg ch – 18{24-30} sts (not counting sl sts) and 6{8-10} ch-2 sps.

Row 2: Ch 4 (counts as first tr) turn, tr in next 2 sts, *ch 2, sk next ch-2 sp, sc in next 3 sts, ch 2, sk next ch-2 sp, tr in next 3 sts; rep from * to last 2 ch-2 sps, sk next ch-2 sp, tr in next st; leave rem sts unworked – 16{22-28} sts and 4{6-8} ch-2 sps.

Size S/M Only

Row 3: Turn, sk first st, sl st in next 3 sts, ch 2, sk next ch-2 sp, tr in next 3 sts, ch 2, sk next ch-2 sp, sc in next 3 sts, ch 2, sk next ch-2 sp, tr in next 3 sts, ch 2, sk next ch-2 sp, sc in next st, sc2tog (worked over next st and top of turning ch) – 11 sts (not counting sl sts) and 4 ch-2 sps.

Row 4: Ch 3 (does not count as a st), turn, sk first st, tr in next st, ch 2, sk next ch-2 sp, sc in next 3 sts, ch 2, sk next ch-2 sp, tr in next 3 sts, ch 2, sk next ch-2 sp, sc in next 3 sts; leave rem sts unworked – 10 sts and 3 ch-2 sps.

Row 5: Ch 4 (counts as first tr), turn, tr in next 2 sts, ch 2, sk next ch-2 sp, sc in next 3 sts, ch 2, sk next ch-2 sp, tr in next 3 sts, ch 2, sk next ch-2 sp, sc in next st; leave turning ch unworked – 10 sts and 3 ch-2 sps.

Row 6: Ch 1, turn, sc2tog (working over first sc and next ch-2 sp), ch 1, sc in next 3 sts, ch 2, sk next ch-2 sp, tr in next 3 sts, ch 2, sk next ch-2 sp, sc in next 2 sts, sc in top of turning ch – 10 sts and 2 ch-2 sps.

Row 7: Ch 4 (counts as first tr), turn, tr in next 2 sts, ch 2, sk next ch-2 sp, sc in next 3 sts, ch 2, sk next ch-2 sp, tr in next 2 sts, tr2tog (working over next 2 sts, skipping the ch-1 sp between them) – 9 sts and 2 ch-2 sps.

Row 8: Turn, sl st in first st, ch 1, sc2tog, ch 2, sk next ch-2 sp, tr in next 3 sts, ch 2, sk next ch-2 sp, sc in next 2 sts, sc in top of turning ch – 7 sts and 2 ch-2 sps.

Row 9: Ch 4 (counts as first tr), turn, tr in next 2 sts, ch 2, sk next ch-2 sp, sc in next 3 sts, ch 2, sk next ch-2 sp, tr in last st – 7 sts and 2 ch-2 sps.

Row 10: Ch 1, turn, sk first st and ch-2 sp, tr in next 3 sts, ch 2, sk next ch-2 sp, sc in next 2 sts, sc in top of turning ch – 6 sts and 1 ch-2 sp.

Row 11: Ch 4 (counts as first tr), turn, tr in next 2 sts, ch 2, sk next ch-2 sp, sc in next 3 sts – 6 sts and 1 ch-2 sp.

Row 12: Ch 4 (counts as first tr), turn, tr in next 2 sts, ch 2, sk next ch-2 sp, sc in next 2 sts, sc in top of turning ch – 6 sts and 1 ch-2 sp.

Row 13: Ch 3 (counts as first dc), turn, dc in next 2 sts, ch 1, sk next ch-2 sp, sc in next 2 sts, sc in top of turning ch – 6 sts and 1 ch-1 sp. Fasten off.

Size L/1X Only

Row 3: Turn, sk first st, sl st in next 3 sts, ch 2, sk next ch-2 sp, tr in next 3 sts, *ch 2, sk next ch-2 sp, sc in next 3 sts, ch 2, sk next ch-2 sp, tr in next 3 sts; rep from * to last ch-2 sp, ch 2, sk next ch-2 sp, sc in next 2 sts, sc in top of turning ch – 18 sts (not counting sl sts) and 6 ch-2 sps.

Row 4: Ch 4 (counts as first tr), turn, tr in next 2 sts, *ch 2, sk next ch-2 sp, sc in next 3 sts, ch 2, sk next ch-2 sp, tr in next 3 sts; rep from * to last 2 ch-2 sps, sk next ch-2 sp, tr in next st; leave rem sts unworked – 16 sts and 4 ch-2 sps.

Row 5: Ch 1, turn, sk first st, sc in next 3 sts, ch 2, sk next ch-2 sp, tr in next 3 sts, ch 2, sc in next 3 sts, ch 2, sk next ch-2 sp, tr in next 3 sts, ch 2, sk next ch-2 sp, sc in next tr, sc2tog (working over next st and top of turning ch) – 14 sts and 4 ch-2 sps.

Row 6: Ch 3 (does not count as a st), turn, sk first st, tr in next st, *ch 2, sk next ch-2 sp, sc in next 3 sts, ch 2, sk next ch-2 sp, tr in next 3 sts; rep from * across – 13 sts and 4 ch-2 sps.

Row 7: Ch 1, turn, sc in first 3 sts, ch 2, sk next ch-2 sp, tr in next 3 sts, ch 2, sc in next 3 sts, ch 2, tr in next 3 sts, ch 2, sk next ch-2 sp, sc in next st; leave turning ch unworked – 13 sts and 4 ch-2 sps.

Row 8: Ch 1, turn, sc2tog (working over first sc and next ch-2 sp), ch 1, sc in next 3 sts, ch 2, sk next ch-2 sp, tr in next 3 sts, ch 2, sk next ch-2 sp, sc in next 3 sts, ch 2, sk last ch-2 sp, tr in last 3 sts – 13 sts and 3 ch-2 sps.

Row 9: Ch 1, turn, sc in first 3 sts, ch 2, sk next ch-2 sp, tr in next 3 sts, ch 2, sk next ch-2 sp, sc in next 3 sts, ch 2, sk next ch-2 sp, tr in next 2 sts, tr2tog (working over next 2 sts skipping the ch-1 sp between them) – 12 sts and 3 ch-2 sps.

Row 10: Turn, sl st in first st, ch 1, sc2tog, ch 2, sk next ch-2 sp, tr in next 3 sts, ch 2, sk next ch-2 sp, sc in next 3 sts, ch 2, sk next ch-2 sp, tr in next 3 sts – 10 sts and 3 ch-2 sps.

Row 11: Ch 1, turn, sc in first 3 sts, ch 2, sk next ch-2 sp, tr in next 3 sts, ch 2, sk next ch-2 sp, sc in next 3 sts, ch 2, sk last ch-2 sp, tr in last st – 10 sts and 3 ch-2 sps.

Row 12: Ch 1, turn, sk first st and ch-2 sp, tr in next 3 sts, ch 2, sk next ch-2 sp, sc in next 3 sts, ch 2, sk next ch-2 sp, tr in next 3 sts – 9 sts and 2 ch-2 sps.

Row 13: Ch 1, turn, sc in first 3 sts, ch 2, sk next ch-2 sp, tr in next 3 sts, ch 2, sk next ch-2 sp, sc in last 3 sts – 9 sts and 2 ch-2 sps.

Row 14: Ch 3 (counts as first dc), turn, dc in next 2 sts, ch 1, sk next ch-2 sp, sc in next 3 sts, ch 1, sk next ch-2 sp, dc in last 3 sts – 9 sts and 2 ch-1 sps.
Fasten off.

Size 2X/3X Only
Row 3: Turn, sk first st, sl st in next 3 sts, ch 2, sk next ch-2 sp, tr in next 3 sts, *ch 2, sk next ch-2 sp, sc in next 3 sts, ch 2, sk next ch-2 sp, tr in next 3 sts; rep from * to last ch-2 sp, ch 2, sk next ch-2 sp, sc in next 2 sts, sc in top of turning ch – 24 sts (not counting sl sts) and 8 ch-2 sps.

Row 4: Ch 4 (counts as first tr), turn, tr in next 2 sts, *ch 2, sk next ch-2 sp, sc in next 3 sts, ch 2, sk next ch-2 sp, tr in next 3 sts; rep from * to last 2 ch-2 sps, sk next ch-2 sp, tr in next st; leave rem sts unworked – 22 sts and 6 ch-2 sps.

Row 5: Turn, sk first st, sl st in next 3 sts, ch 2, sk next ch-2 sp, tr in next 3 sts, *ch 2, sc in next 3 sts, ch 2, sk next ch-2 sp, tr in next 3 sts; rep from * to last ch-2 sp, ch 2, sk last ch-2 sp, sc in next st, sc2tog (working over next st and top of turning ch) – 17 sts and 6 ch-2 sps.

Row 6: Ch 3 (does not count as a st), turn, sk first st, tr in next st, *ch 2, sk next ch-2 sp, sc in next 3 sts, ch 2, sk next ch-2 sp, tr in next 3 sts; rep from * to last 2 ch-2 sps, ch 2, sk next ch-2 sp, sc in next 3 sts; leave rem sts unworked – 16 sts and 5 ch-2 sps.

Row 7: Ch 4 (counts as first tr), turn, sk first st, tr in next 2 sts, *ch 2, sk next ch-2 sp, sc in next 3 sts, ch 2, sk next ch-2 sp, tr in next 3 sts; rep from * to last ch-2 sp, ch 2, sk last ch-2 sp, sc in next st; leave turning ch unworked – 16 sts and 5 ch-2 sps.

Row 8: Ch 1, turn, sc2tog (working over first sc and next ch-2 sp), ch 1, sc in next 3 sts, *ch 2, sk next ch-2 sp, tr in next 3 sts, ch 2, sk next ch-2 sp, sc in next 3 sts; rep from * across working last sc in top of turning ch – 16 sts and 4 ch-2 sps.

Row 9: Ch 4 (counts as first tr), turn, tr in next 2 sts, ch 2, sk next ch-2 sp, sc in next 3 sts, ch 2, sk next ch-2 sp, tr in next 3 sts, ch 2, sk next ch-2 sp, sc in next 3 sts, ch 2, sk next ch-2 sp, tr in next 2 sts, tr2tog (working over next 2 sts skipping the ch-1 sp between them) – 15 sts and 4 ch-2 sps.

Row 10: Turn, sl st in first st, ch 1, sc2tog, ch 2, sk next ch-2 sp, tr in next 3 sts, ch 2, sk next ch-2 sp, sc in next 3 sts, ch 2, sk next ch-2 sp, tr in next 3 sts, ch 2, sk next ch-2 sp, sc in next 2 sts, sc in top of turning ch – 13 sts and 4 ch-2 sps.

Row 11: Ch 4 (counts as first tr), turn, tr in next 2 sts, ch 2, sk next ch-2 sp, sc in next 3 sts, ch 2, sk next ch-2 sp, tr in next 3 sts, ch 2, sk next ch-2 sp, sc in next 3 sts, ch 2, sk last ch-2 sp, tr in last st – 13 sts and 4 ch-2 sps.

Row 12: Ch 1, turn, sk first st and ch-2 sp, tr in next 3 sts, ch 2, sk next ch-2 sp, sc in next 3 sts, ch 2, sk next ch-2 sp, tr in next 3 sts, ch 2, sk next ch-2 sp, sc in next 2 sts, sc in top of turning ch – 12 sts and 3 ch-2 sps.

Row 13: Ch 4 (counts as first tr), turn, tr in next 2 sts, ch 2, sk next ch-2 sp, sc in next 3 sts, ch 2, sk next ch-2 sp, tr in next 3 sts, ch 2, sk next ch-2 sp, sc in last 3 sts – 12 sts and 3 ch-2 sps.

Row 14: Ch 4 (counts as first tr), turn, tr in next 2 sts, ch 2, sk next ch-2 sp, sc in next 3 sts, ch 2, sk next ch-2 sp, tr in next 3 sts, ch 2, sk next ch-2 sp, sc in next 2 sts, sc in top of turning ch – 12 sts and 3 ch-2 sps.

Row 15: Ch 3 (counts as first dc), turn, dc in next 2 sts, ch 1, sk next ch-2 sp, sc in next 3 sts, ch 1, sk next ch-2 sp, dc in next 3 sts, ch 1, sk next ch-2 sp, sc in next 2 sts, sc in top of turning ch – 12 sts and 3 ch-1 sps.
Fasten off.

FINISHING

Sew shoulder and side seams.

Armhole Edging

From RS, join yarn with sl st at side seam of armhole.

Rnd 1: Ch 1, work 72{80-88} sc as evenly spaced as possible around armhole edge; join with sl st in first sc.

Rnd 2: Ch 1, sc in each sc around; join with sl st in first sc.
Fasten off.

Rep around other armhole.

Outer Edging

From RS, join yarn with sl st in first st of back neck.

Rnd 1: Ch 1, sc in same st as joining, work 24 sc spaced as evenly as possible across back neck, work 48{54-60} sc spaced as evenly as possible across edge to marker at front corner, 3 sc in marked sp, move marker to center sc of the 3-sc group just made, work 107{143-179} sc spaced as evenly as possible across edge to next front corner marker, 3 sc in marked sp, move marker to center sc of the 3-sc group just made, work 48{54-60} sc spaced as evenly as possible across edge to beg of rnd; join with sl st in first sc – 234{282-330} sc.

Rnd 2: Ch 4 (counts as first tr), 6 tr in same st as joining, (sk next 3 sts, sc in next st, *sk next 2 sts, 7 tr in next st, sk next 2 sts, sc in next st; rep from * to 3 sts before first marker, sk next 3 sts, 11 tr in marked st) twice, sk next 3 sts, sc in next st, **sk next 2 sts, 7 tr in next st, sk next 2 sts, sc in next st; rep from ** to last 3 sts, sk last 3 sts; join with sl st in top of beg ch.
Fasten off.

Ties (work 2)

From RS, join yarn with sl st in marked front corner, ch 72.
Fasten off.

Rep on opposite front corner.

Weave in ends.

QUICK COCOON

EASY +

SIZE

About 42" x 38" (106.5 cm x 96.5 cm), before folding and seaming

SHOPPING LIST

Yarn (Medium Weight) MEDIUM 4

LION BRAND® HEARTLAND® (Art. #136)

- ☐ #350 Mount Rainier Tweed - 8 balls **or** color of your choice

Crochet Hook

LION BRAND® crochet hook

- ☐ Size J-10 (6 mm) **or** size needed for gauge

Additional Supplies

- ☐ LION BRAND® stitch markers
- ☐ LION BRAND® large-eyed blunt needle

GAUGE

12 sts = about 4" (10 cm) over Rows 1-3 of Wave pattern.
BE SURE TO CHECK YOUR GAUGE.

NOTES

1. A rectangle of fabric is crocheted in Wave pattern, then folded and seamed to make the Cocoon.
2. Stitches of different heights create a wavy design.
3. Edging is worked around front edge.

COCOON

Ch 128.

Wave Pattern

Row 1: Working in back bumps of ch, hdc in 3rd ch from hook (2 skipped ch do not count as a st), dc in next 4 ch, *hdc in next 2 ch, sc in next 4 ch, hdc in next 2 ch, dc in next 4 ch; rep from * to last ch, hdc in last ch – 11 waves.

Row 2: Ch 2 (does not count as a st), turn, working through back loops only, hdc in first hdc, sc in next 4 dc, *hdc in next 2 hdc, dc in next 4 sc, hdc in next 2 hdc, sc in next 4 dc; rep from * to last st, hdc in last hdc.

Row 3: Ch 2 (does not count as a st), turn, working through back loops only, hdc in first hdc, dc in next 4 sc, *hdc in next 2 hdc, sc in next 4 dc, hdc in next 2 hdc, dc in next 4 sc; rep from * to last st, hdc in last hdc.

Rep Rows 2 and 3 until piece measures about 38" (96.5 cm) from beg.

FINISHING

Note: There is no right or wrong side to the crochet piece. Just use the side you like best for the right side!

Fold piece in half to measure 21" x 38" (53.5 cm x 96.5 cm).

Place markers on each of the 21" (53.5 cm) sides, 7" (18 cm) below fold for armholes. Seam sides from armhole markers down to lower edge.

Front Edging

Rnd 1: From RS, join yarn with a sl st in front edge at center of one long edge, ch 1, *sc in end of next row, 2 sc in end of next row; rep from * around to work sc evenly spaced all the way around the front opening; join with sl st in first st.

Rnd 2: Ch 1, turn, working through back loops only, sc in each st around; join with sl st in first st.

Rep Rnd 2 until edging measures about 4" (10 cm).

Weave in ends.

GENERAL INSTRUCTIONS

ABBREVIATIONS

beg = begin(ning)(s)
ch = chain
ch-sp(s) = chain space(s) previously made
cm = centimeter
dec = decreas(e)(s)(ing)
dc = double crochet
hdc = half double crochet
mm = millimeters
rem = remain(ing)(s)
rep (s) = repeat(s)
RS = right side
rnd(s) = round(s)
sc = single crochet
sk = skip
sl st = slip stitch
sp(s) = space(s)
st(s) = stitch(es)
tog = together
tr = treble (triple) crochet
WS = wrong side

* — When you see an asterisk used within a pattern row, the symbol indicates that later you will be told to repeat a portion of the instruction. Most often the instructions will say, repeat from * so many times.

( ) or **[ ]** — Sets off a short number of stitches that are repeated or indicates additional information.

— When you see – (dash) followed by a number of stitches, this tells you how many stitches you will have at the end of a row or round.

CROCHET HOOKS																	
U.S.	B-1	C-2	D-3	E-4	F-5	G-6	7	H-8	I-9	J-10	K-10½	L-11	M/N-13	N/P-15	P/Q	Q	S
Metric - mm	2.25	2.75	3.25	3.5	3.75	4	4.5	5	5.5	6	6.5	8	9	10	15	16	19

CROCHET TERMINOLOGY		
UNITED STATES		INTERNATIONAL
slip stitch (slip st)	=	single crochet (sc)
single crochet (sc)	=	double crochet (dc)
half double crochet (hdc)	=	half treble crochet (htr)
double crochet (dc)	=	treble crochet (tr)
treble crochet (tr)	=	double treble crochet (dtr)
double treble crochet (dtr)	=	triple treble crochet (ttr)
triple treble crochet (tr tr)	=	quadruple treble crochet (qtr)
skip	=	miss

Yarn Weight Symbol & Names	LACE 0	SUPER FINE 1	FINE 2	LIGHT 3	MEDIUM 4	BULKY 5	SUPER BULKY 6	JUMBO 7
Type of Yarns in Category	Fingering, size 10 crochet thread	Sock, Fingering, Baby	Sport, Baby	DK, Light Worsted	Worsted, Afghan, Aran	Chunky, Craft, Rug	Super Bulky, Roving	Jumbo, Roving
Crochet Gauge* Ranges in Single Crochet to 4" (10 cm)	32-42 sts**	21-32 sts	16-20 sts	12-17 sts	11-14 sts	8-11 sts	6-9 sts	5 sts and fewer
Advised Hook Size Range	Steel*** 6 to 8, Regular hook B-1	B-1 to E-4	E-4 to 7	7 to I-9	I-9 to K-10½	K-10½ to M/N-13	M/N-13 to Q	Q and larger

*GUIDELINES ONLY: The chart above reflects the most commonly used gauges and hook sizes for specific yarn categories.

** Lace weight yarns are usually crocheted with larger hooks to create lacy openwork patterns. Accordingly, a gauge range is difficult to determine. Always follow the gauge stated in your pattern.

*** Steel crochet hooks are sized differently from regular hooks–the higher the number, the smaller the hook, which is the reverse of regular hook sizing.

BEGINNER	Projects for first-time crocheters using basic stitches. Minimal shaping.
EASY	Projects using yarn with basic stitches, repetitive stitch patterns, simple color changes, and simple shaping and finishing.
INTERMEDIATE	Projects using a variety of techniques, such as basic lace patterns or color patterns, mid-level shaping and finishing.
EXPERIENCED	Projects with intricate stitch patterns, techniques and dimension, such as non-repeating patterns, multi-color techniques, fine threads, small hooks, detailed shaping and refined finishing.

GAUGE

Never underestimate the importance of gauge. Achieving the correct gauge assures that the finished size of your piece matches the finished size given in the pattern.

CHECKING YOUR GAUGE

Work a swatch that is at least 4" (10 cm) square. Use the suggested hook size and the number of stitches given. If your swatch is larger than 4" (10 cm), you need to work it again using a smaller hook; if it is smaller than 4" (10 cm), try it with a larger hook. This might require a swatch or two to get the exact gauge given in the pattern.

METRICS

As a handy reference, keep in mind that 1 ounce = approximately 28 grams and 1" = 2.5 centimeters.

TERMS

fasten off — To end your piece, you need to simply cut and pull the yarn through the last loop left on the hook. This keeps the last stitch intact and prevents the work from unraveling.

right side — Refers to the front of the piece.

LION BRAND® HEARTLAND®

Article #136
Weight Category: 4 - Worsted Weight: Afghan, Aran Yarn
Solids: 5oz/142g (251yd/230m)
Tweeds: 4oz/113g (200yd/183m)
Solids: 100% Acrylic
Tweeds: 94% Acrylic, 6% Rayon

Gauge:

Knit: 16 sts + 22 rows = 4 inches on size 9 [5.5 mm] needles
Crochet: 12 sc + 15 rows = 4 inches on size J-10 [6 mm] hook

Product Care Instructions: Items made from this yarn may be machine laundered only on the setting designed for gentle agitation and/or reduced time for delicate items. Any dry cleaning solvent other than trichloroethylene may be safely used. No bleach product may be used. A machine dryer may be regularly used at a maximum of Low Heat setting. Item may not be smoothed or finished with an iron.

VISIT LionBrand.com FOR:

- Learn to Knit & Crochet Instructions
- Weekly newsletter with articles, tips, and updates
- Store Locator

We have made every effort to ensure that these instructions are accurate and complete. We cannot, however, be responsible for human error, typographical mistakes, or variations in individual work.

Copyright © 2015 by Leisure Arts, Inc., 104 Champs Blvd., STE 100, Maumelle, AR 72113-6738, www.leisurearts.com. All rights reserved. This publication is protected under federal copyright laws. Reproduction or distribution of this publication or any other Leisure Arts publication, including publications which are out of print, is prohibited unless specifically authorized. This includes, but is not limited to, any form of reproduction or distribution on or through the Internet, including posting, scanning, or e-mail transmission.

©2015 Lion Brand® Yarn Company, all rights reserved.

Made in U.S.A.